Fighters Blood

Regina Rose

BookLeaf
Publishing

India | USA | UK

Presentation by *BookLeaf Publishing*

Web: www.bookleafpub.com

E-mail: info@bookleafpub.com

ISBN : 9789357447935

First edition 2021

DEDICATION

To everyone who always kept believing in me and never gave up hope. Because of your support I was able to get through it all. You know who you are and what you mean to me.

From the bottom of my heart, thank you.

PREFACE

Enjoy the rollercoaster I call my life.

The start

We are all born naked.
No one ever has a clue,
what we are supposed to do.
No idea why we are here,
or what our purpose is going to be.

But you, you could never protect me.
From all the demons in my head.
All the monsters crawling underneath my bed.
All the darkness that dragged me in their trap.
"Does anybody have a map?"
How to deal with this child?
Who always smiled.

Our baby used to be so small.
Trying so hard to keep her out deaths arms.
But everything was said to a wall.
And all she wanted was to take her last breath.

The Male Enemy

Always drunk,
so much luggage in your trunk.
Needed the alcohol to speak,
because sober you were too weak.
Too weak to talk about life,
or even talk to your wife.
Drowning yourself in your sorrow.
Not caring about tomorrow.
Not looking at the pain and hurt you caused.
What if life got paused?

A little girl,
Standing before you with tears as pearls.
Do you hear yourself scream?
Do you hear the sound of that girl's dream?
She just wanted to create some winter fun.
But you shoot your words through her heart like
a gun.
She never meant any harm.
There is the alarm.

Your time is up.
So did your behaviour let you win the World
Cup?
Did this pause change anything?

Because that little girl is your daughter and she
desperately holds on to that one little string.
The string you give her sometimes.
But also take away, because of her "crimes".
Your string of love is running short.
Stop drinking! Drinking is not a sport!

The Female Enemy

"I'm back from school!
Can I go to the swimming pool?"
Where is she?
Could it be?
Carefully I go upstairs.
I walk closer while the world prepares.
Bloodstains on the floor.
I open the door…

"GET OUT OF YOUR BED YOUNG LADY!"
Was it a dream maybe?
Or just my never-ending nightmare?
Getting some rest will forever be so rare.
So I look into her eyes.
I'm so afraid that soon she will die.

Fantasy World

I build a world full of magic,
because my world was tragic.
I felt like Alice in Wonderland.
With so many friends on each hand.
There was no worry in the sky
and I ate so much apple pie!
That made me so happy.
That I even named myself Abbey.
Who was the girl from that tragic world?
When everything I ever wished for, could be
built.
My castle, a fountain of cheese, dogs for
everyone!
Every bad person got none.
No sun, because I love the snow.
It gives me that wonderful glow.
Running around, not stressed about tomorrow.
Just feeling free from all the sorrow.
This is the place I will spend most of my days.
This place deserves so much praise.

The Loved ones

Despite the loneliness I felt
and all the pain I dealt with.
I had amazing people surrounding me.
Both still owning a special key.
To my heart and my mind.
They always treated me kind.

Always eating an egg sandwich,
or a huge bread bun.
They weren't rich,
but it was always fun.
They made sure I became strong.
Gave me the tools to grow from a girl into a
woman.
With great talks, but also just a silly song.
That's how I would become zen.

These two are truly the best.
And I'm so blessed,
with them helping me fight the bears I need to
face.
Holding me in their warm embrace.
There is no other place I would rather be.
Then in the arms of she.

Black out

I have no idea where I am.
Do I even give a damn?
I have no idea how I are.
Do I need to know how far?
I have no idea where I go.
Do I need to know?

I am walking in the dark.
Searching for a spark.
In this huge space of nothingness.
Feeling the loneliness.
Growing stronger and bigger every minute.
What would be in it?

I feel like fading away.
I don't want to play.
Mommy, daddy, are you there?
Do you even care?
Your child, laughing but dying inside.
Living in a fantasy where she hides.

Your child is not here.
She wants to disappear.
She is hiding in her mind.

Do you dare to reach out to her, are you ready
for what you will find?
Well, you have nothing to worry about.
Cause she is having a black out.

The Rope

The rope hanging on the ceiling.
Life has no meaning.
The pain is just too much.
I just needed a simple touch.
Just a warm hug,
but all I got was an uninterested shrug.
With the rope around my neck,
there is no turning back.
I wanted a way out
and I'm so freaking proud.
Cause this was my choice.
And with this they could finally hear my voice.

Ready to take this leap of faith.
At only the age of eight.
Do they see me now?
Taking my final bow…

But the older one walks in and I survive.
Why did Mr. Destiny keep me alive?

Help

Now I'm sitting here in the waiting room.
Waiting for this rollercoaster of doom.
Was my attempt worth all this trouble?
I was happy being in my bubble.
Hiding and not wanting to be seen.
Now I'm sitting here in between,
the two biggest enemies in my life.
Waiting for this person to talk about our strife.
How to speak freely when the problem is them?

I am just a kid.
I should've learned from what ever they did.
Now I am here,
how is everything going there on the rear?
No focus, stay.
There has to be a way,
to go back into the shadows.
Nobody is allowed to know, that's how it goes.

A note from future me

Come little girl, take my hand.
I will take you to a magic land.
You will be able to control water.
You'll be a hero, the perfect daughter.
In here they cannot hurt you.
Believe me when I say, you will make it
through.
You don't want it yet.
But with all the people you've met.
Life is going to be amazing.
Life is going to be so fascinating.

So hush now small girl,
Roll yourself in a curl.
Hold on, soon there will be no shouting
anymore.
You're gonna win this war.
There are so many beautiful humans.
They are there, no made up mutants.
Take your blanket and go to sleep.
How it hurts me to hear you weep.

Hopefully your dreams will be sweet.
I will be with you every heart beat.

Dear tiny version of me,
By the time you get to read this, you will be free.
I know where you came from,
and I know the woman you will become.
You will become fierce and strong.
And you've finally found where you belong.
No longer hiding or seeking the truth.
You will be no longer holding a grudge against
your youth.
In the future there will be loads of sunshine.
I know about the hurt, how we almost left when
we were eight, but trust me when I tell you that
wasn't our time.

Hey

Hey there,
I know it's dark wherever you are.
And I know we got loads of stuff to repair.
You are going to win this war.

Hey little one,
I know you feel like you're done.
But please don't give up, go on.
At the end of the road will be a new dawn.

Hey beautiful,
You're not going crazy, you're not getting
delusional.
There is truly light at the end.
Shining bright, made by a friend.

Hey lovely,
Don't listen to them who only speak ugly.
Walk to that bright light your friend is showing.
And I promise you'll start glowing.

Hey there little beautiful lovely girl,
You are the most beautiful Pearl.
Each day you keep on improving.
You just need to keep on moving.

Youngest

The oldest makes you feel so small.
She is like the stepsister of Cinderella, and
you're not allowed to go to the ball.
She always knows best.
She is always better than the rest.

The world gave her a hard time.
That's why your existence is like a crime.
She saved your life back then, but what for?
So she could only hurt you more?
Rip your heart out and push it into the ground.
Didn't she see the two enemies drowned you.

But no, she is so good,
And never did any harm.
She was the one made from the best wood.
3th one is definitely not the charm.
Last best, rephrase that into first best.
You always made me the odd one in the nest.

Living like a Puppet

No rhymes for today, cause I'm a Puppet and
I'm not able to do so.
People play with me.
Without knowing about my true feelings.
Because some puppeteer painted a smile on my
face.
I can't have an other face or show any other
emotion.
This is how I am made.
The puppeteer attached some strings on me.
So you can make me dance,
You can make me fall.
You can put me in every position you like.
And do to me whatever you wish.
Because you will never hear the voice of a
puppet who doesn't want to be played with.

Sex

I was way too young.
My life had just begun,
but you believed my lies.
You could never see my eyes.
I wrote all those stories and you just simply
believed,
while you were getting deceived.
But who cared about that, you just followed your
dick.
Not caring about my true feelings, you prick.

But you knew, you knew my age,
You got to feel the middle's one rage.

You wanted a family,
and you thought you could build that with me.
My age wasn't important,
so when it happend I just went dormant.
For a whole year I kept it all a secret.
After that I could not longer keep it.
All the pain I caused myself, that was now
enough.
I hope this is what you're still thinking of.
May you feel as miserable as I was after you
came.

I truly hope you'll drown in your misery, cause
I'm not the one to blame.

And you knew all of this.
Yet you touched me without my permission.
It's frustrating that it's you I still miss.
Why did you bring us in this position?

So much unwanted sex.
It felt like a hex.
And now I'm living with all the defects.
But that's okay, cause I'm free and safe now.
And no man nor woman will ever touch me
without my permission, that's my final vow.

Stairs

I threw myself of the stairs today.
Cause I wanted to fade away.
And my soul wants to fly,
but the gods never send a reply.

I hear them running.
I can feel my back burning.
Even when the floor is cold.
Do you think this was bold?

The female enemy comes from upstairs and the
male enemy from downstairs.
Do they know or are they unaware?
Will they care if I told them this hurt was caused
by I?
Or will they hate me for this lie?

They help me stand on my feet,
and help me to a seat.
They help, they care, but why don't I feel their
love, am I not capable of this feeling?
What are they truly meaning?

"I'm okay"
is what I abruptly say.

"I'm not your daughter, don't love me.
Don't care for me, I just want to be free.

That's why I threw myself of the stairs today."

Don't go

Don't ever dare to say,
that you are okay.
When it's all a lie,
and you want to die.
See me as your light.
Cause I will be there for you every night.
And when your smile will disappear,
when no one is near.
I will know what you hide.
I don't want you to go to the other side.
I see you are smiling,
but I know you are lying.
You have the right to cry,
so please my darling, don't say goodbye.

Pixie

I was sixteen when we met,
and that is the day I will never forget.
It was love at first sight,
and you became my light.
I had my death figured out the day after that
festival.
You made me feel incredible.
You stopped me from taking those pills the
Monday after.
Just by making me die of laughter.
You sparked a little light on the inside.
And that light has never died.
You gave me strength, you didn't want the
strings of that old puppet.
"Without the strings and it's me you'll get."
that's what you said.
You showed me how to love myself and set
boundaries.
And I'm holding on to those memories.
We're not together,
but that's for the better.
I do still care about you,
And I truly hope you're happy with whatever
you do.

And I will hold our memories dear to my heart,
written in my Rose tattoo.

22

Nakama

Alongside Pixie there were some orcs, pirates
and mages.
All accepting me for who I am.
And oh damn.
I never expected to get a new family like them.
Every single one of them is such a beautiful
gem.
They are one bunch of crazy, but that's fine.
They were my sign,
the sign to not give up on living.
To start giving.
To not give up, but to fight.
They never left my side.
They gave me so much love and so much
support.
Together, we build our fort.
Hurt one of us and we will hunt you down.
I just come from a small town.
Just a small loving family, nothing to complain.
But this extra family freed me from my chain.

Emotions

I'm so sick of people telling me I'm too
emotional.
My emotions are like voices, screaming non stop
at me, so uncontrollable.
My head is always running.
In the night I feel my heart turning.
Even though she sometimes doesn't want to deal
with my head.
How about you try to live like this for a day
instead?
Give me some peace and quiet.
Instead of this continuing riot.
I'm trying to run away from it.
Please, just give me a break,
and I will admit:
I made a mistake.
I'm sorry my head doesn't always do what I
want.
I can't be cool or nonchalant.
That's not in my DNA.
I'm constantly grinding in my head, everyday.
I'm tired, yet always talking,
jumping, flying and walking.
If you could walk in my shoes,
Would you do it without any bruise?

Will you still complain about me being all over
the place?
Or will you look me in the face,
and tell me that it's okay to be a little extreme.
I'm just blowing off a little steam.

Sorry send to Heaven

I was a little thief,
and the oldest loved one gave me the relief.
But I never got to say sorry to the other oldest.
I don't even know if you ever noticed.
The money missing from the tray.
I still feel bad about it to this day.
I promised myself to give it back.
But I lost track.
And I don't know how much I owe,
but you've already gone below.
So I'm never able to pay.
But I can only pray,
pray for you to hear me asking for your mercy.
And that you will set me free.
I'm sorry for what I've done.
And I'm sorry I didn't tell you before you were
gone.
Dear grandmother up there in the sky.
I wish I could fly.
To hear your voice telling me it's okay.
I hope this poem will be able to reach you in
some way.

The Enemy

At the end of the day, you're sitting alone.
Your heart feels like stone.
You're trying to figure out if everything was
real,
but living with amnesia makes that a very hard
deal.
You try so hard to remember,
but your mind is so dark as an ember.
Screaming from inside, trying to get the
memories back.
But it stays black.

There's one little light.
It's very bright.
Very hard to see,
but I know it's meant for me.
I'm still searching for the right answers,
so I took my chances.
I jumped,
and I bumped.

Back in black,
feeling like a wreck.
Will this nightmare stop?
….with a single teardrop

I get pushed back into reality.
Was it just a different personality?
In the end, the conclusion I've learned is: "The
real big fat mega Enemy…"
"Will always be me."

Dear future Me

Dear future me,
you must be thirty-three.
That's 10 years from now.
Did you keep your vow?
How's life up there?
Did it get easier to bear?

I won't bother you with too many questions my
dear.
I hope you get to live without fear.
I hope you still surround yourself with good
people,
and that you finally find yourself equal.
Equal to everyone, that you also deserve love
and someone who cares.
I hope you got fewer bears,
on the road of life.
I truly hope the most you haven't touched the
knife.
That means you're 11 years clean!
Hopefully that is not just a dream.

I hope that you can look into the mirror and say:
"I'm pretty,bitch."
Cause that attitude will make you rich.

I tell you, mark my words.
At least… that's what I was told by the big birds.
I hope you're okay with being different from the rest,
and that you finally realise you're truly blessed.
Cause I've learned that no matter how deep I sink into the mud.
I've got fighters blood.